WHAT'S THE BIG IDEA?

OPPOSITES

Pamela J.P. Schroeder
Jean M. Donisch

ROURKE PUBLICATIONS, INC.
VERO BEACH, FL 32964

A book by Market Square Communications Incorporated.
A special thanks to our creative team, Sandy Robinson, Sandra Shekels and
Ann Garber of Market Square Communications Incorporated, for their creative
text and design contributions.

Consultants:
> Jeanette Handrich — M.A. in Elementary Education/Language Arts,
> third and fourth grade teacher/gifted and talented program,
> over 20 years teaching experience
>
> Karen M. Olsen — M.S. in Education, kindergarten teacher, over 20
> years teaching experience
>
> Geri Pape — M.S. in Elementary Education, kindergarten teacher,
> over 30 years teaching experience

Library of Congress Cataloging-in-Publication Data
Schroeder, Pamela J.P., 1969-
  Opposites / Pamela J.P. Schroeder, Jean M. Donisch.
    p.   cm. — (What's the big idea?)
  Summary: An introduction to the study of opposites presented
through the use of rhyme.
  ISBN 0-86625-579-6
  1. English language—Synonyms and antonyms—Juvenile
literature. [1. English language—Synonyms and antonyms.]
I. Donisch, Jean M., 1960-   . II. Title. III. Series.
PE1591.S39   1996
428.1—dc20   96-735
                                                      CIP
                                                      AC

Printed in the U.S.A.

TABLE OF CONTENTS

For more fun with OPPOSITES ideas, look for this shape on the page.

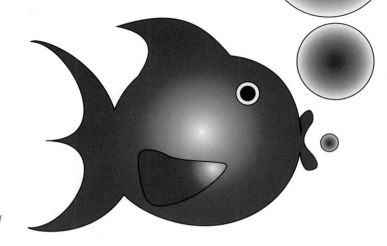

WHAT'S THE BIG IDEA?

ABOUT OPPOSITES

In this book
About opposite pairs,
There are big ideas only —
No small ones to spare.

Hot and cold, front and back,
Left and right, thin and thick —
For any idea you might have
There is an opposite.

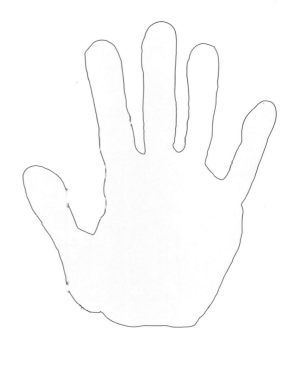

To every beginning
There is an end.
We start out as strangers,
But then become friends.

Open this book and start to read.
Close it when you're done.
Take what's inside out with you,
And you'll have some fun.

Left

You can write with your left hand, or write with your right.
Your right shoe might fit your left foot, but it's tight.

Right

Are most kids in your class left-handed or right-handed?

Point right with your left hand, and point left with your right. Now you're all crossed in the middle. It must be quite a sight!

Open

What things do you wish stayed open all the time?

COOKIE JAR

Open the door to let the sun shine in.
If it's raining, you'll have to close it again.

8

Closed

When the cookie jar is open, you can reach for the sweets.
When the cookie jar's closed, you can't get the treats.

In

ERNEST IN THE MUSIC BOX

When can you be in and out at the same time?

You can stay in your house or go out on the town.
In comes together and out spreads around.

10

Out

"Put your toys in your box," means put them away.
Take them out again and it's time to play!

up

12

Down

If you climb up a tree you can get to the top.
If you climb down, the ground is where you'll stop.
Up is the sky where fireworks pop.
Down is the ground, at the end of a hop.

What does it mean when you're feeling up? Feeling down?

Near

Far is away, down the street — off you go.

Near is up close. It can mean toe to toe.

Far

Is near an inch, a meter, a yard?
Does a mile, or two, or 100 mean far?

How near, or how far away, does your best friend live?

Front

The front is the face side, the part that comes first.
The back comes in second. It's no better or worse.

Back

How do you tell the front of a candy bar from the back?

Front and back are connected. You can't shake them loose.
Everyone's face is in front, and in back's the caboose.

Little

Seahorses are little and don't take up much space.
Whales are big and spread out all over the place.

Big

What things would make a whale seem little?

A big fish in a little pond might be the boss.
A little fish in a big pond just might get lost.

Thin

What kind of present might be in a thin box?

Thin is a string, a needle and thread.
Thick is like yarn, for the hat on your head.

Thick

Many thin things together can make something thick.
Split a thick thing apart — you'll get thin out of it.

Empty

If you had a jar that would stay full all the time, what would you want in it?

Empty means nothing is inside at all.
Full is up to the top, no matter how tall.

22

Full

Full can get empty if what's in gets out.
Put something back in — that's what full's all about.

Few

What are
some things
you would only
want a few of?

If you have a few, you don't have lots.
That's good, if you're talking about chicken pox.

24

Many

If you have many points, it means you've won the game.
Piles of money or marbles can mean the same.

Hot

It's hot in the jungles and deserts, you know.
It's cold at the north pole where there's always snow.

Cold

What temperature means it's a hot day?

Hot soup sure feels good on a cold winter day.
Cold lemonade keeps the hot of summer away.

ABOUT OPPOSITES

In this book
About opposite pairs,
There were big ideas only —
No small ones to spare.

Hot and cold, front and back,
Left and right, thin and thick —
For any idea you might have
There is an opposite.

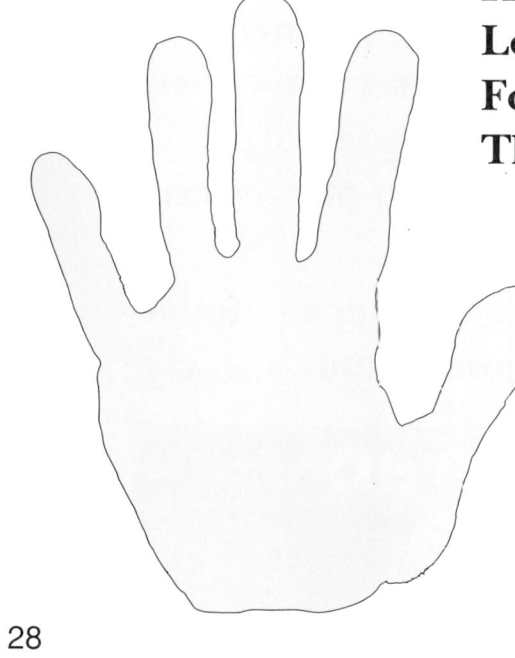

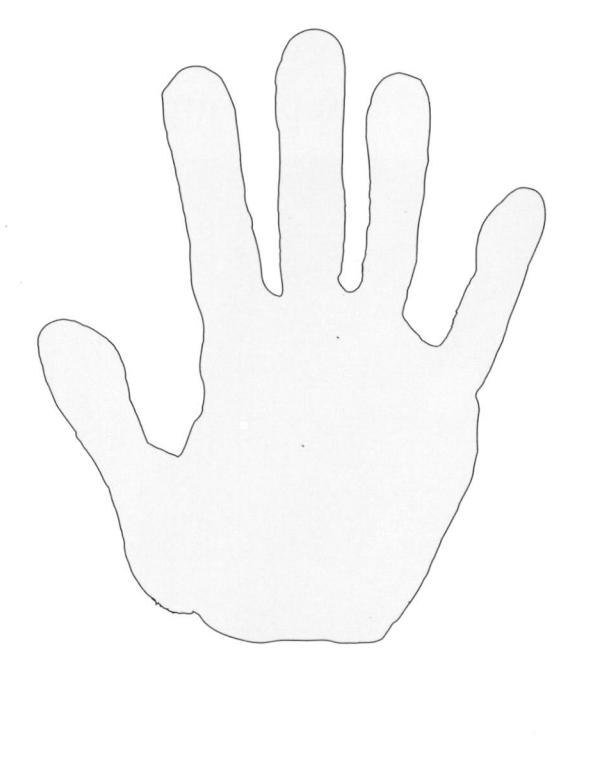

You opened this book to start reading.
You'll close it when you're done.
Take what's inside out with you,
We hope you've had some fun.

You started at the beginning
And now it is the end.
We started out strangers,
And now we are friends.

GLOSSARY
OF OPPOSITE PAIRS

few – a small number of things; not many

many – a large number of things; not few

front – the face; the part of something that faces
    forward

back – the part behind the front; the part of
    something that faces backward

hot – having a high temperature; the sun is hot

cold – having a low temperature; ice is cold

in – inside, held by something

out – outside, away from something

left – the opposite direction of right; if you stick
    out your thumbs and look down at the back of
    your hands, the left hand makes an "L"

right – the opposite direction of left; most people
    write with their right hands

little – small in size; not big
big – of great size, large; not small

near – close, a short way away; not far
far – a long way away; not near

open – able to get inside; not closed
closed – not able to get inside, shut

opposite – different in every way
same – the opposite of opposite

thin – not much space between sides; thread is thin
thick – lots of space between sides; yarn is thicker
    than thread

up – away from the ground, from a lower to a
    higher place
down – toward the ground, from a higher to a
    lower place

ABOUT OPPOSITES

How many opposite pairs can you name for the sizes of things?

What words besides little are the opposite of big?

With your friends, make up a skit to show someone the opposites in this book.

What colors have opposites?

What would a person who is the opposite of you be like?

What feelings can you name that have opposites?

What does it mean when people say, "Friends stick by each other through thick and thin"?

Would you rather have few or many brothers or sisters? Why?

What things are better hot? What things are better cold?